The Elisha Factor:
Living the Double-Portion Life

A DEVOTIONAL

KEVIN P. HORATH

LUCIDBOOKS

THE ELISHA FACTOR
Living the Double-Portion Life: A Devotional
Copyright © 2018 by Kevin P. Horath

Published by Lucid Books in Houston, TX
www.LucidBooksPublishing.com

eISBN-10: 1-63296-213-6
eISBN-13: 978-1-63296-213-3
 ISBN-10: 1-63296-212-8
 ISBN-13: 978-1-63296-212-6

Special Sales: Most Lucid Books titles are available in special quantity discounts. Custom imprinting or excerpting can also be done to fit special needs. Contact Lucid Books at Info@LucidBooksPublishing.com.

To Mom and Dad:
Thank you for teaching and demonstrating these factors.
Congratulations on celebrating 55 years of pastoral ministry.

To Breanna, Cody, Norah, Penelope, and Henry:
Thank you for creating the awesome cover for this book.
I hope the inside lives up to the outside. I am so proud of you all.

To Camden:
You are an amazing son. I am proud of who you are and of who you are becoming. I am blessed to have you in my life.

To Joe and Andrea:
You have demonstrated true friendship. You guys are truly an inspiration to me.

To my amazing wife, Kathy:
You have taught me to laugh again. Thank you for inspiring and encouraging me to write this book. Even if you didn't know what to say, you would make up a word. I love you.

For Willetta:
You are celebrating in heaven now. Thank you for preserving my thoughts from my blog onto your website so many years ago. Without it, I would have experienced more difficulty creating this book. I miss our talks.

Table of Contents

Foreword

I believe *The Elisha Factor* was written for such a time as this. In 2 Corinthians 11:3 NIV, God's Word says something profoundly basic, nevertheless utterly essential to living a victorious Christian life. Paul cautions that we not allow the enemy any opportunity to "lead our thoughts astray from sincere and pure devotion to Christ." It's clear. The Apostle Paul is saying devotion to God begins in our thought life. I know it's true for me. My thinking forms my attitudes, creates my perceptions about my circumstances, and ultimately determines my ability to obey God in my daily life. I guess that's why, as long as I can remember being a Christian, I have used daily devotionals as my first defense of each day to "order my thoughts aright." It is literally a battle of the mind!

Through the years, I've accumulated an assortment of devotional books. However, as I have come to see our world heading fast into the most perilous times in which I remember living, I have also come to realize my need for the meat of God's Word as never before. While the enemy's deceptive cunning increases, the warrior of Christ must stand vigilant with a sound mind saturated by daily time in the Spirit-breathed Words of Scripture. A daily devotional book is always a great tool for getting into the Word. However, too much of current Christian literature is driven by a market looking to sell a product. Platitudes of positive thinking written to make you feel good about yourself are the goal for most devotional books today. But, friends, flowery words alone seldom reach the core and change you. You must go into the deepest places of the heart. You must be challenged to confront your true self and look into the mirror of God's Word. Not only that, living now in a time when the enemy comes in like a flood with all manner of lies, God's people must raise a standard and a clarion voice of truth. We must go out with the armor of God strapped on securely. To be in the Word with a concentrated dose of spiritual nutrition is required for our daily victory. Herein is exactly why I believe, *The Elisha Factor*, by Kevin Horath, has come into my daily devotional life for such a time as this.

I have known Kevin and his family for many years. I have also been privileged to know many of the great men and women of God who have helped shape Kevin's life. When Kevin writes in this devotional about the need for healthy relationships within the Church, it is because he has seen firsthand how critical this need is for the successful function of any local Church, and he has had his own life touched intimately by the outcomes of this dynamic. When Kevin writes in chapter 4 about the "theologies" of the Holy Spirit, he is able to make it plain to understand. That's because Kevin has been taught and exposed to the intricacies of Biblical doctrine since his youth. I remember that Kevin knew more of doctrinal truths as a teenager than most adults I knew. His is a seasoned knowledge of the myriad of approaches people take to being "filled with the Spirit." Having a lifetime of practical ministry experience, this is just one example of how this devotional book tackles what are often complex issues and puts them into easy-to-understand terms. And when Kevin writes, "If more Christians would really live holy lives (and not holier-than-thou lives) in business, school, church, and home, revival would literally break out across the United States and around the world," I am compelled to humble myself before the presence of a Holy God and seek His face for my own personal revival. This is what a devotional book should do.

I was honored being asked to write this foreword to a book I myself have now come to love. It has met and exceeded my hunger for a daily devotional that gives me the meat of God's Word, taking me deeper into my daily walk with God. I will use it again and again. My challenge to you is to read ahead now and do the same. Make a daily time to use *The Elisha Factor* to help you saturate your thoughts each day in the Word, setting your thoughts aright, and winning the battle of the mind.

Joe Stricklin
Evangelist, Songwriter, and Friend

Introduction

So many factors influence our lives. Recognizing these factors is vitally important. Therefore, this devotional is the by-product of a sermon series I preached entitled, *The Elisha Factor*. This series focused on the life and ministry of Elisha, an Old Testament prophet who followed in the footsteps of Elijah. His story can be found in 1 Kings and 2 Kings. We often hear sermons and messages about Elijah, a fiery, if not moody, prophet. However, Elisha is not mentioned quite as much. Yet, as we will see, there are a lot of factors to learn from this important prophet. This devotional will systematically take a look at much of his life and ministry, starting with his call, ending with a miracle that took place after his death, and covering much more in between.

One of the things I like to do when studying Scripture is to try and understand the smallest details. Sometimes amazing truths and deep insights can be found in those details. In Scripture, we find names are very meaningful. Elisha's name is no different as there is great meaning and significance in his name. Proverbs 22:1 says:

> *A good name is rather to be chosen than great riches, and loving favour rather than silver and gold.*

In order to understand his name, we have to break it down. We can do this by looking at some other Scripture verses. While being crucified, the Bible records seven specific phrases uttered by Jesus. One of those phrases can be found in Matthew 27:46. Jesus cried:

Eli Eli lama sabachthani?

This literally means, "My God, my God, why hast thou forsaken me?" We know this because Scripture gives us the interpretation in the very same verse. "Eli" means "My God." That part is fairly easy to deduce.

The last part of Elisha's name is "sha." This is a shortened form of the word, "shu'a," which means "salvation." When we put these words together, we see that Elisha's name literally means, "My God is Salvation."

The name "Elisha" is a shortened form of "Elishua" and was a common Old Testament name. In fact, David had a son with the same name (2 Sam. 5:15; 1 Chron. 14:5). "Elishua" is very similar to "Joshua" or "Yahshua," which means, "Yahweh is Salvation." Another pronunciation for "Yahshua" that we use today is "Jesus." This will come as no surprise as we begin to see the similarities and typologies between Elisha (My God is Salvation) and Jesus (Yahweh is Salvation).

For comparison, Elijah's name means, "My God is Yahweh." I find these small facts very interesting and helpful in my study. I know I can be geeky sometimes, but that's me.

Anyway, Elijah, the forerunner of Elisha, was a rugged prophet. In contrast, Elisha was a gentle prophet of vision. Each was unique in their respective ministries and both were needed in their respective times. We often hear about the need for more "Elijahs" today and I certainly agree with that statement. However, I also want to submit for consideration that we need more "Elishas." The lessons we can learn from his life and ministry are relevant and vitally important to the Christian life.

You may use this devotional for individual study, small group sessions, Sunday School classes, or even for sermon notes. Some Scriptures will be printed for you and some are not. Regardless, I encourage you to look up *all* the Scriptures. Dig in for yourself.

Join with me as we consider the Elisha factor.

Factor One:
Called and Equipped

1 KINGS 19:15–21

In addition to anointing kings, God instructed Elijah to anoint Elisha as a prophet. These were some of the duties commonly assigned to Old Testament prophets. Elijah completed these duties, and in this passage we find that Elisha is both called and equipped to serve in the office of a prophet.

Right away, it seems to me that Elisha is an unlikely person for God to call. He was an unassuming person out plowing a field. He seems kind of . . . ordinary. Compared to the fire and brimstone style of Elijah, Elisha seems downright boring. How could God use such a simple person? It does not seem very logical. Despite what we may think about people, Scripture is full of examples of God using the "least of these" in ministry. After all, it is His ministry. He calls and He equips and, quite frankly,

He knows exactly what He is doing. As such, He can use you and He can also use me.

Elijah understood this. He did exactly as God commanded as he delivered the call to Elisha. The Bible does not record any exchange of words when the call was given, yet it tells us that Elijah delivered the message with a sign. 1 Kings 19:19 says:

> . . . and Elijah passed by him, and cast his mantle upon him.

Even without any words spoken, the call to Elisha was clear. There was no mistaking it because it was definite, even though God did not speak directly to Elisha. The call came through Elijah. That is not really all that unusual. However, God does speak directly to us at times. I sincerely believe that. Samuel and Isaiah both heard the voice of God calling them to their respective ministries. Saul (later Paul) received a direct call from Jesus on the road to Damascus. Therefore, God will sometimes speak to us directly. At other times, He will use people to speak on His behalf. No matter how it comes, when it comes we will know. If it is from God, it will be clear. We just need to be open to hearing the call.

Scripture does not tell us if Elisha had a desire to become a prophet, let alone to work in the ministry in any capacity. But, it does show us that Elisha was faithful in what he was doing. He was engaged in the *present* task, his current assignment. His mind was on what he was doing.

Whether he wanted to be in the ministry really doesn't matter. What does matter is that if he did desire this call, it was obvious that he did not take it upon himself to become a prophet. He was faithful in the task assigned to him and did not take the next step until he was called. In fact, I wonder if Elisha could have been a little annoyed. I mean, think about it. He was working hard and some wise guy came along and threw a mantle on him, without even saying a word! My first response would probably be, "Hey, I'm workin' here!" But, that's me.

Elisha, however, somehow understood exactly what was happening, and he left the oxen and ran after Elijah. He worked faithfully at his job and did not attempt to enter the ministry until God called him. When God called him, through Elijah, Elisha took the next steps. He understood the call.

We, too, need to understand the call. It is easy to get caught up with the need, the opportunity, our abilities, and even our desires. These things very well may exist, but they are not the call. The need is not the call, having an opportunity is not the call, our skill is not the call, and our desire to be in ministry is certainly not the call. God's call is the call. We must wait for it and stop trying to get ahead of God, even if we have a burning desire to be in His service.

I experience that desire. Perhaps you do, too. The call is amazing. Although, do not allow yourself to be fooled. Ministry is not meant to be glamorous. The call involves difficult work. I am sure plowing the field was hard work, too. However, life was about to get a bit harder for Elisha in a lot of different ways. Following the Lord is a difficult task—at least as far as the natural man is concerned. It is not all sunshine and rainbows. Once you respond to God's call, expect to be involved in spiritual warfare. You can expect trouble, tribulation, and persecution. Jesus warned His disciples (and us) that this will happen. He was right. Yet, He does not leave us unprepared.

God always equips us for His service. He does not leave us hanging and He does not forsake us. He will never call us and then just leave it up to us to figure out what to do next. Elijah demonstrated the equipping of God by placing his mantle upon Elisha. This was not a practical joke played on a man who was working hard. No, this was representative of the anointing of the Lord, and it was a serious thing. When God calls us, He will fully equip us with what we need.

Therefore, do not become confident in your own abilities because God is not impressed by them. Neither should you be worried about your disabilities because God is not concerned by what you cannot do. He just needs your availability. That is what He wants and that is exactly what He will use.

Elisha was available. He responded with a whole-hearted surrender and he was prepared to leave everything to follow the Lord. Yet, when we compare his response to Luke 9:61–62, we see what, on the surface, may appear as a contradiction. This passage states:

> *And another said, Lord, I will follow thee; but let*
> *me first go bid them farewell, which are at home*

at my house. And Jesus said unto him, No man, having put his hand to the plough and looking back, is fit for the kingdom of God.

Why was it all right for Elisha to say goodbye to his family but it was not all right for the person who would follow Jesus? Careful study of Scripture reveals an important point Jesus was trying to make. Earlier, in Luke 9:54, Jesus's disciples tried to compare Jesus with Elijah. They wanted Jesus to call fire down from heaven like Elijah did. In fact, many people thought Jesus *was* Elijah. Remember when He asked His disciples about this? You can find this incident recorded in Luke 9:18–20. Peter got the answer right. He understood that Jesus was not Elijah.

He said unto them, But whom say ye that I am?
Peter answering said, The Christ of God.
—Luke 9:20

As the Book of Hebrews instructs us, Jesus is better than Moses, better than the prophets (Elijah), and better than the angels. This comparison of Jesus to Elijah is not even close. It was all right for Elisha to say goodbye to his family and then follow Elijah. However, Jesus is better than Elijah. When He calls, we go. Period.

Also, the reference in Luke 9:62 should be noticed again. It says:

And Jesus said unto him, No man, having put his hand to the plough and looking back, is fit for the kingdom of God.

What was Elisha doing when Elijah called him? He was plowing. This is a mirrored metaphor that Jesus is using. Elisha left his plowing to follow Elijah and Jesus utilizes plowing as a metaphor to follow Him. The Jews would have picked up on this reference immediately and with all of the talk of Elijah in Luke 9, they should have understood the difference.

So should we. God calls and equips. When He does, we go. However, that is not the end of the story.

It is just the beginning.

Factors to Consider:

1. What does your name mean? Does this meaning describe characteristics about you? How can God use these characteristics in ministry for Him?

2. What about your life makes you feel ordinary and not useful to God? Now think about how God can use an "ordinary you" and describe what that might look like.

3. Have you received a call from God in your life? If so, how do you know it?

4. How have you been faithfully serving God right now and right where you are today?

5. What keeps you from serving God wholly and completely?

Factor Two:
Inheriting the Double Portion

2 KINGS 2:1–14

History indicates that Elisha spent perhaps somewhere between seven and nine years ministering to and learning from Elijah. As 2 Kings 2 begins, it is clear that the time had come for Elijah to leave his earthly ministry. Before this happened, though, Elisha had some final tests to complete.

This, perhaps, is one of my favorite stories in Scripture. I like it because it really shows the need and, dare I say, the requirement of relationships in ministry. Relationships are extremely important! This particular story shows deep love with undying commitment. It also shows true respect. From my limited experience in ministry, I see that the Church still needs to learn and incorporate these lessons. We do not always do transitions in ministry correctly. Elisha, on the other hand, handled it perfectly and we can learn so much from him. We *need* to learn so much from him.

The first eight verses of this chapter show there were numerous opportunities for Elisha to step away from Elijah. Perhaps Elisha could have gone off and begun his own ministry at this time. Elijah was taking a final "victory lap" and he gave Elisha the chance to stay behind. However, Elisha would not have any of this. His dedication and love were evident in his passionate response:

> As the LORD liveth, and as thy soul liveth, I will not leave thee.
> —2 Kings 2:2

That is loyalty. Had Elisha left Elijah at this point, he would have missed out on the most important blessing of his life. Sure, he still could have had a successful ministry and he still could have done great things for the Lord. But, there is a vital lesson here. His love for Elijah *mandated* that he stay until the very end. Even his response to the other prophets informing that Elijah's time was short tells us of his deep love for Elijah. Elisha replies:

> Yea, I know it; hold ye your peace.
> —2 Kings 2:3

Even though great things were ahead for Elisha, he knew his earthly relationship with Elijah was coming to a close. There was a lot of history with Elijah. And this, I believe, was hard, naturally, for him to accept. He did not want Elijah to leave. He enjoyed their time together. Therefore, he wanted to spend each moment possible with him. He wanted to see this through—all the way to the end.

Regarding relationships in the Church, we do not always see them through to the end. A more accurate statement is that we probably end them prematurely. In some respects, we have become too much like secular enterprise in that ministry is no longer personal; it is business. Do not misunderstand me. There are things that need to be conducted in a business-like manner. However, leaders and potential leaders sometimes grab, grasp, and claw at every opportunity to get to the next level in the Church. I have seen it happen over and over. Some say, "God has called me to this or that so I will do everything possible to make that happen." This attitude comes with the risk and potential cost of hurting others! These individuals may even be "successful" from a worldly perspective as they move up the ladder.

Yet, I wonder what we leave on the table when we try to move up in our own power and timing. Elisha, as we learned in the last chapter, knew better than to do this. He was faithful in his current assignment (whether plowing fields or learning from Elijah) and he did not try to force God into the next step. He patiently waited for the right time—God's time.

As the end drew near, Elijah granted Elisha a final request. In response, Elisha asked for a "double portion of thy spirit" to be granted to him (2 Kings 2:9). I have heard, in my opinion, numerous misunderstandings of this particular request. Some say that Elisha was asking to be twice as effective in ministry as Elijah. They claim this is evident because there are twice as many miracles recorded for Elisha as there are for Elijah. However, in my study, I have trouble accepting this premise.

Let me explain. I have often heard exciting phrases that sound good (and perhaps even Biblical) like, "I want a double dose of the Holy Ghost!" I mean, that sounds good, right? We like our "bumper sticker theology" and our memes that play well on Twitter and Facebook! We get all excited when someone utters that phrase or something similar in Church. We laugh and say, "Yeah, that's what I want, too." We get goose bumps and a double dose sounds like a great thing to desire. But, is this scripturally sound? I am not trying to be judgmental or overly critical. I want the best for us and I want us to understand Scripture and spiritual concepts correctly. Can we get "more" of the anointing on our life? Or, do we get all of the Holy Spirit when we are saved and live for Him?

I do not think we can get *more* of God. I have not found any Scripture that bears this out. He has already given us His all! Although, I do believe He can get more of us. We do need to yield to Him and walk with Him and allow Him to fill us (Gal. 5:25). But, that is not what I see happening here in this passage.

Rather, I believe Elisha was simply asking to be the rightful heir of Elijah's ministry. Consider Deuteronomy 21:17:

> *But he shall acknowledge the son of the hated for the firstborn, by giving him a double portion of all that he hath: for he is the beginning of his strength; the right of the firstborn is his.*

This passage tells us that the firstborn was to get a double portion of the inheritance. What does this mean?

Think of it this way. If a man has two sons, his wealth (money, property, etc.) would be divided into thirds. The firstborn would get two-thirds (a double portion) and the other son would get one-third. Altogether, this represents 100% of the inheritance. If a double portion means that the firstborn would get twice as much (or 200%) as the father, how could that be possible? Can a man bequeath more than he owns? Of course not! Therefore, I do not believe that is what Elisha is requesting, either. His request is to be the recognized firstborn heir to the ministry of Elijah among all the other prophets.

Here is where we need some further understanding and where we see some amazing connections to who Jesus is and to who we are in Him. We now understand the importance of the birthright from Deuteronomy 21:17. We can also see the importance of the birthright as found in Genesis 25 with Jacob and Esau. If you take some time to read that story, you may find it valuable. It shows the importance of being the firstborn as the rightful heir in order to receive the double portion (birthright).

Once that is understood, consider Jesus. Colossians 1:15 tells us that He is the firstborn of all creation. Additionally, Romans 8:29 tells us that Jesus is the firstborn among many brethren. All things are under His feet, according to Ephesians 1:20–23, and Jesus is, therefore, entitled to the double portion by inheritance. Hebrews 1:3–4 sums it up by saying:

Who being the brightness of his glory, and the express image of his person, and upholding all things by the word of his power, when he had by himself purged our sins, sat down on the right hand of the Majesty on high: Being made so much better than the angels, as he hath by inheritance obtained a more excellent name than they.

Jesus is the firstborn. That is indisputable. He has the right of the double portion. Elisha, then, is a typology of Jesus. But, wait, there is more! This is where it gets really exciting. John 1:12 tells us that we have the power (right, authority) to become the sons of God, also. Normally, that does not give us the same right as the firstborn. We would just be other children, like the other prophets in Elisha's day, and not eligible for the double portion. But, Romans 8:14–17 tells us that if we are adopted children of God, we are now heirs of God. Hold on. That's not all. We are not just heirs, but we are *"joint-heirs"* with Christ. Romans 8:17 says:

And if children, then heirs; heirs of God, and joint-heirs with Christ; if so be that we suffer with him, that we may be also glorified together.

When we are born again, we are adopted into the family of God and we are entitled to the double portion. It is not something else we need to ask for or earn. Through Christ, it is now our birthright, too. We have our inheritance in Him (Eph. 1:11–14). When we trust Him, we are sealed, or authenticated, by the Holy Spirit.

The Holy Spirit is the earnest of our inheritance that we receive *right now*. The earnest is a pledge. It is a portion or a part of the thing purchased as a pledge that we have the whole. Jesus purchased our salvation and we have been established, anointed, and sealed with the earnest of the Spirit! 2 Corinthians 1:21–22 says:

Now he which stablisheth us with you in Christ, and hath anointed us, is God; Who hath also sealed us, and given the earnest of the Spirit in our hearts.

Therefore, when we trust Jesus as our Savior, we have the double portion inheritance, too. We do not need to ask for more of Him. We have Him. His Spirit has been given to us as the earnest of the inheritance we will ultimately receive in Glory one of these days!

We do not need more of God because we already have the double portion when we are born again. This should really excite us. It is time to understand this truth and begin moving out in this authority and inheritance. Why are we wasting time asking for the double portion when we already have it?

Elisha was simply asking to be the rightful heir of Elijah. However, it is not that simple. He asks a hard thing (2 Kings 2:10). It is not hard for God to award but it is a hard thing to inherit. There is a lot of responsibility and there is also a lot of trouble ahead. It was true for Elisha, and it is true for us. If this is really what God wanted for Elisha, then Elijah was willing to leave it in God's hands by God allowing Elisha to see him taken away. Yes, it was up to God. But, it was up to Elisha, too. He played a part and things immediately began to happen.

As they were walking, a chariot of fire appeared. It came between Elijah and Elisha and it physically parted them. I wish that the only way we can be separated from one another today is by an act of God. That was the only way Elijah and Elisha could be parted. No promise of ministry, no promise of success, nothing on earth could come between them. It took an act of God to separate them.

That is what I want to see in the Church. Instead, we are often separated by perceived slights, petty fights, and our own so-called spiritual wisdom. We allow things, often silly things, to come between us when instead it should take an act of God to separate us. That doesn't mean a person must die or be taken away before we step out into ministry. But, we do need to make sure it is an act of God—the call of God—that sends us out into our new role. Unfortunately, I have seen too many examples of fame, ego, fortune, and other fleshly desires separate those working together in ministry. What a lesson there is here for us to learn!

When Elijah was taken away, Elisha cried, "My father, my father, the chariot of Israel, and the horsemen thereof." Again, I see the analogy of father and son, solidifying my belief that the double portion is representing Elisha becoming the rightful heir. Again, the double portion is not a double anointing. God's anointing is enough. We do not need *more* anointing when we have *the* anointing on our lives.

Elisha then did something else that I find very important. He tore his own clothes into two pieces and he picked up the mantle that fell from Elijah. He approached the river Jordan and asked, "Where is the LORD God of Elijah?" This was not a question of doubt. No, this was a question of faith. I find it very interesting that he still invoked the name of Elijah. Elijah was gone and this was supposed to be the era of Elisha. It is a new day! Why remember Elijah? Elisha understood the necessity to honor and respect those who have gone before. Jeremiah 6:16 says:

> *Thus saith the LORD, Stand ye in the ways, and see, and ask for the old paths, where is the good way, and walk therein, and ye shall find rest for your souls. But they said, We will not walk therein.*

Elisha understood this principle, and he asked for the old path, the way of Elijah. The people in Jeremiah's day did not. I think we do not understand this completely today, either. We do owe a lot to those who have blazed the trail before us. Just because they are gone does not mean they are forgotten and everything they have done gets wiped away. The world might do that. The Church must not.

Elisha tore his own garments because this was not about him. He was in mourning in a natural sense. He picked up the mantle—Elijah's mantle—and he ran with it. Why? Because he was the rightful heir. He entered the ministry the right way. Spiritually, he was ready. Elisha knew what it meant to inherit the double portion.

He also understood the power of the double portion. I am glad we do, too.

Factors to Consider:

1. What rights or privileges do the firstborn or only child have that the rest of the children do not have?

2. Explain the concept of the "double portion" as you now understand it.

3. Is it possible to "get more of God" or more anointing in your life? If so, what scripture bears that out? If not, is it possible to "give God more" of ourselves? If so, what scripture bears that out?

4. Think back to a time in your life when you felt the urge to be independent of your parents. Were you ready to leave when you left? What lessons could you have gained by remaining until you were truly ready to leave?

5. What about the role of the Church to equip us to minister to others? What would happen if you left the influence of your spiritual parents before you had all the tools you needed?

Factor Three:
Handling Insults and Conflict

2 KINGS 2:23–24

"Once you go bald, there is no growing back!" "You know you are going bald when it takes you longer and longer to wash your face in the morning."

"Why wouldn't the bald man let anyone use his comb? Because he couldn't part with it."

Oh, I could keep going. There are a million of them and I have probably heard every one! Being hair-follicly challenged myself, I am not unfamiliar with the bald jokes. I hear them just about every day and I am now used to it. Hey, I even participate in it!

As we continue studying the life of Elisha, we come to one passage that my own kids have always thought was very, very funny. 2 Kings 2:23 says:

> *And he went up from thence unto Bethel: and*
> *as he was going up by the way, there came forth*

little children out of the city, and mocked him, and said unto him, Go up, thou bald head; go up, thou bald head.

Funny, right? Well, verse 24 explains what happens next. Elisha turned around and called down a curse in the name of the Lord. Immediately, two she-bears came out of the woods and 42 of the boys were savagely mauled.

Whoops! Did we read that correctly? Is Elisha such a cranky old man that he cannot handle some little children who are just being kids? What is happening in these verses? I mean, really, this seems a bit harsh. Right?

As always, we have to look closely at Scripture, and we need to let Scripture interpret itself whenever possible. For instance, how old are these "little children"? Some might say "little children" would refer to those up to 10 years old. Others say that the translation should read "young lads," which would indicate they may have been up to 20 years old. How do we really know what is going on?

Let's look to another Scripture for help. In the following text, the prophet Samuel asked Jesse if all of his children were present. We read in 1 Samuel 16:11:

And Samuel said unto Jesse, Are here all thy children? And he said, There remaineth yet the youngest, and, behold, he keepeth the sheep. And Samuel said unto Jesse, Send and fetch him: for we will not sit down till he come hither.

Jesse said that the "youngest" was not present. David was "the youngest of Jesse's children." How old was

David at this time? Just a few verses later, 1 Samuel 16:18 says that David was a "mighty valiant man" and also calls him a "man of war." This would suggest that he was not a small child. Rather, he was probably a young man. He could have been 20 years old or maybe even older.

Therefore, it could be that these "little children" who mocked Elisha were not little kids as we might think of little children today. They were most likely of a responsible age and old enough to know what they were doing. They were, I believe, young men. They lived in Bethel, where there was a golden calf erected by Jeroboam. Bethel had become a stronghold of idolatry and a center of apostasy. It appears that these young men were representative of a wicked movement that blasphemed the name of God (Bethel means "House of God"). Therefore, their attack on Elisha was not just kids being kids. It was the outward expression of a determined, rebellious attitude against God.

But still, this story still seems a bit sadistic, vicious, and cruel. What did these offenders do to deserve such judgment? Well, we must remember, Elisha was God's prophet. That's right—*God's* prophet. These young men were representatives of their false gods. Since Elisha was the representative of the One True God, the attack against him was really an attack against God. We can read the New Testament verse in Acts 9:4 that reveals this truth:

> *And he fell to the earth, and heard a voice saying unto him, Saul, Saul, why persecutest thou me?*

When Saul persecuted the early Christians, he was really persecuting the Lord Jesus! The Lord called Saul on this. The same thing is happening in this situation with Elisha and these young men.

The term "bald head" that these young men used was an expression of abuse—an insult. They also said, "Go up." Why did they say this? Was it because they knew Elijah had just gone up and, in effect, were telling Elisha to go away, too? It seems to me that this was a challenge to the power and authority of God. That challenge is about to be met—game on! The problem is that this is not a game. No, it is about to get as real as it can get.

Elisha simply turned around, looked at them, and cursed them in the name of the Lord. Notice that he did not curse at them, as some of us might want to do. As a result of the curse, bears immediately came out of the woods and mauled them. They paid an awful price for their rebellion against God.

Was Elisha wrong to do this? Jesus rebuked His disciples for wanting to call down fire (Luke 9:54). Jesus told us that we are to bless those who curse us and speak all manner of evil against us. We are to bless them, not curse them. Nevertheless, the proof that this curse was not wrong is the fact that God backed up what Elisha said. We know this because He sent swift and terrible judgment.

So, what do we do today? Is this a contradiction in Scripture? Frankly, I believe we need to heed Jesus's words. Elisha was an Old Testament prophet and lived in a different time. Jesus came and fulfilled the Law. Just as it was all right for Elisha to say goodbye to his parents before following Elijah, it was all right for him to pronounce this curse. However, when it is time to follow Jesus, we do not have the luxury of waiting. Furthermore, we must follow His example of love. Luke 9 is packed full of examples of Elijah and Jesus, yet we should remember that Hebrews tells us that Jesus is "better" than the prophets. The bar was raised. The Law was fulfilled. We are now under the New Testament. We must leave vengeance to the Lord (Rom. 12:19).

What do we learn from this? If we are not to respond in the same manner as Elisha, why bother studying this particular incident? Is it just to try and scare our young people when they misbehave? No, I think we learn the following:

1. We must not have a distorted view of God. Yes, God is love, but He is also a God of judgment.
2. God cannot be defied forever. Defying God is a dangerous thing to do and it comes with dangerous consequences.
3. It is also very dangerous to persecute God's people. When we do, we are persecuting Jesus Himself.

How we handle conflicts and insults is very important. Elisha did what he had to do. Today, we are called to a higher standard. We love our enemies. We bless those who curse us. Jesus made this very clear:

> Bless them that curse you, and pray for them which despitefully use you.
> —Luke 6:28

That is how you handle conflicts and insults.

Factors to Consider:

1. How do you respond when someone insults you or challenges you?

2. Romans 12:19 tells us not to avenge ourselves because vengeance belongs to the Lord. Therefore, does that mean we should rejoice when our enemies get what we think should be coming to them? Why or why not?

3. Jesus said to do good to those who hate you. What is one way you can bless an enemy of yours?

4. Have you ever spoken badly about your pastor? Could that be considered persecuting God's people? Why or why not?

5. God is a God of mercy and grace. He is also a God of judgment. How can He be all these things? How do we recognize the many characteristics of God in our daily life?

Factor Four:
A Spirit Filled Life

2 KINGS 4:1–7

I believe God's plan and provision for every person is that they should be filled with the Holy Spirit. Period. End of the chapter, right? Well, not so fast.

I know there are differing opinions and theologies regarding what that means and how it happens. I will not get into that discussion so much in this chapter. However, it is a practical, doctrinal position that needs to be understood. Make sure you take the time to do that.

Yet, the Bible is clear that *every* born-again Christian has the Holy Spirit. Inheriting the "double portion" does not mean that we can get more of the Holy Ghost. I do not believe it is more of an anointing on our lives. God's anointing is enough. The double portion represents being the rightful heir. The Bible tells us that we are heirs of God and joint-heirs with Jesus, and we have the Holy Spirit when we are born again. We have learned this already.

However, there is a different experience (and subsequent experiences) that happens when we yield to the Holy Spirit. We often call this the "Filling of the Spirit" and some will call this experience the "Baptism of the Holy Spirit." Perhaps the "Filling of the Spirit" is a better term because the "Baptism of the Holy Spirit" refers to the new birth. 1 Corinthians 12:13 says:

> *For by one Spirit are we all baptized into one body, whether we be Jew or Gentiles, whether we be bond or free; and have been all made to drink into one Spirit.*

But, that is also another topic for another day and, perhaps, another book. Confused yet? Hang in there. In 2 Kings 4:1–7, we find a historical event that can also be used as a parable—an earthly story with a spiritual meaning. When studying parables, we have to be careful not to take the analogies too far. If we do, we can miss the overall point by trying to uncover every minute detail. The goal is to find the overarching theme so we can apply the lesson to be learned.

This story is about a poor widow whose husband had been a servant of the Lord. Her husband died and she was now destitute. She and her children were in danger and they needed some serious help. Elisha, the prophet of God, provided that assistance. After she appealed to Elisha, her small reserve of oil miraculously multiplied enough to fill all her needs. This is an example of how once empty vessels became filled with oil. Oil, in the Bible, is representative of the Holy Spirit. The empty vessels represent our lives. This story shows us how our empty hearts and lives can become Spirit-filled.

Just how can this happen? I am so glad you asked. Here is her story and how we can apply it today.

The widow owned nothing (except a little oil) and had no means of support. The creditors came and demanded payment and even threatened to take her sons as payment. She was in serious trouble, so what did she do? She did a tough thing. She put away her pride. She admitted her poverty to Elisha, the prophet of God. This was an important first step for her. As with any problem, we must admit that it exists.

For some, this is quite difficult, and often times, it is done as a last resort. Many like to be self-sufficient and like to think they can make their own destiny. We may believe that if we just think positive thoughts, we can add to our lives. However, Jesus warns us in Matthew 6:27:

> *Which of you by taking thought can add one cubit unto his stature?*

Jesus is not talking about our height. He is talking about our lives and the amount of time we have on this earth. Our positive thinking cannot add one hour to our lives. Worrying can, no doubt, shorten our lives, but it cannot lengthen it. Therefore, we must directly face the problem. We have to admit that we, without Christ, are empty. We have to recognize that we are in debt without any means to pay that debt.

The widow recognized this in her own life and she realized she needed help. She did not have the means on her own. However, she did have a little something. Although the widow was destitute, she had the oil. As Christians, we have something, too. When we are born again, we have the Holy Spirit (oil). The moment we believe, He is with us. Take a moment to look up and read John 14:16–17 and 1 Corinthians 6:19. Additionally, Romans 8:9–11 says:

> *But ye are not in the flesh, but in the Spirit, if so be that the Spirit of God dwell in you. Now if any man have not the Spirit of Christ, he is none of his. And if Christ be in you, the body is dead because of sin; but the Spirit is life because of righteousness. But if the Spirit of him that raised up Jesus from the dead dwell in you, he that raised up Christ from the dead shall also quicken your mortal bodies by his Spirit that dwelleth in you.*

Therefore, each and every Christian has the Holy Spirit. This is not a matter of feelings. This is recognizing what the Lord has said in His Word. It is believing what He has promised. We must recognize what we have. We possess the "oil."

While we have the Holy Spirit when we are saved, He cannot truly fill us as long as we are full of something else. The widow needed empty vessels to hold the oil. She was even told to go borrow some empty vessels. She needed a lot of vessels. Jesus needs empty vessels, too. He wants to fill us but in order to do so, we need to be empty. When we are empty, Jesus can fill our emptiness with His Spirit. Unfortunately, many Christians have not emptied themselves. They are full already—full of themselves, full of religious tradition, full of pride, or maybe even full of sin. The Holy Spirit can only fill empty vessels. As 2 Corinthians 7:1 says, we need to cleanse ourselves from all filthiness of the flesh and spirit. How can the indwelling Spirit fill a hardened heart? How can the Spirit of Truth fill a heart full of lies? How can the Holy Spirit fill a heart that is not holy? We need to empty ourselves completely in order to be filled.

Then, in order to receive her miracle, the widow had to shut the door. She shut the door on the outside world and had her own private time with God. This is necessary in the Spirit-filled life. Corporate prayer is needful; so is private prayer. In many verses in Scripture (particularly in Acts) we see that the infilling of the Spirit often comes in answer to prayer. Additionally, what happens privately in prayer will often be observed in the open. Matthew 6:6 says:

> *But thou, when thou prayest, enter into thy closet, and when thou hast shut thy door, pray to thy Father which is in secret; and thy Father which seeth in secret shall reward thee openly.*

Take time to pray. Be diligent about it and make it an integral part of your life. Pray at all times, with all kinds of prayer. It is, after all, a vital part of the armor of God found in Ephesians 6. Enjoy corporate times of worship, but do not neglect your private prayer, which is essential to the Sprit-filled life.

The widow followed the instructions that Elisha gave her and received her miracle. I wonder if the maximum that God can fill us is directly proportional to the measure of our obedience. In reality, if we are not *completely* obedient, we really are not obedient at all. If we are not in obedience, we are in rebellion. Rebellion, the Bible tells us, is as sinful as witchcraft (1 Sam. 15:23). As we open up our hearts and live in obedience, God can, and will, fill us with the Holy Spirit.

All of this happens in faith. Without faith, it is impossible to please God (Heb. 11:6). We can do all of the previous steps, but if we do not have faith, we can miss out. We must take God at His Word and trust Him. That means we sometimes have to "put legs on our prayers." We sometimes pray for blessings but sometimes we have to be the blessing. As we step out in faith and do our part, God will do His. God is moving. The problem is that we often are not. Be careful to not get ahead of God, though. There is a time to wait in faith and there is also a time to move in faith. When you spend time with God, you will more easily know the difference.

Finally, the widow had to use what God gave her. So do we. The gifts of the Spirit are not for our selfish enjoyment. They are not so we can get goose bumps and say that we "had church." The filling of the Spirit is being equipped for daily living. It is for the edification and building up of the Church and it can also be a sign to the unbelievers. If we say we are filled with the Spirit and we are not effective in our service for the Lord, then we are in a dangerous place. The Dead Sea is filled, but, there is no outlet. That is why it is dead. We are the same. We need an outlet. As we are filled with the Spirit, we should pour out into the lives of others. The Apostle Paul poured out his life as a drink offering. He also had to be filled.

> *And be not drunk with wine, wherein is excess;*
> *but be filled with the Spirit.*
>
> —Eph. 5:18

We should do no less. That is why we need to continually be filled. And emptied. And filled. And . . . you get the idea, right?

Factors to Consider:

1. What does the "filling of the Spirit" mean?

2. Do all born-again Christians have the Holy Spirit? If so, why is the "filling of the Spirit" important?

3. According to Luke 11:9–13, how does a Christian receive the Holy Spirit?

4. What do you need to empty from your life in order to make room for the filling of the Holy Spirit?

5. What are ways we can become an outlet that allows the Holy Spirit to pour into the lives of others?

Factor Five:
Holiness

2 KINGS 4:8-9

In 2 Kings 4, the story of the woman of Shunem is found. We first read of her in 2 Kings 4:8:

> *And it fell on a day, that Elisha passed to Shunem, where was a great woman; and she constrained him to eat bread. And so it was, that as oft as he passed by, he turned in thither to eat bread.*

Why did this "great woman" want Elisha to be welcomed in her home? Why did she feel the need to provide lodging for him? What was so unique about Elisha that this woman and her husband provided so much hospitality to him? I think the very next verse (2 Kings 4:9) tells us why:

> *And she said unto her husband, Behold now, I perceive that this is an holy man of God, which passeth by us continually.*

Elisha was not just a "man of God." No, this woman noticed that he was a "holy man of God." What's the difference? Is there a difference? If so, how do people describe us? Do others call us holy men and women of God? They should, if we are truly Christians, because God requires that we should live holy lives. Not only does God require it, but He also makes it possible. For in and of ourselves, we are not holy because our righteousness is like filthy rags. We need Him because He is holy. 1 Peter 1:15–17 says:

> *But as he which hath called you is holy, so be ye holy in all manner of conversation; Because it is written, Be ye holy; for I am holy. And if ye call on the Father, who without respect of persons judgeth according to every man's work, pass the time of your sojourning here in fear.*

We will explore the furnishing of a believer in the next chapter. However, for now, I want to spend a little time on holiness. What does holiness mean? We often equate it with a list of things to do and things we are not to do. We think of sacrificing physical comforts for spiritual benefits. For some, "holiness" conjures up images of old-fashioned tent meetings, gospel quartets, extremely modest dress, and strong warnings against drinking, dancing, and playing cards.

Today, in the so-called postmodern Church, we have replaced these images of old-fashioned holiness with the practical teachings of financial stewardship, positive thinking, some church attendance, hosting small home group sessions, having moderation in all things, and displaying overall basic morality.

All of these things, whether old-fashioned or modern, can be good and worthwhile pursuits, but they are not the definition of holiness. They just are not. You may have convictions about these things and that is okay. Just be careful and do not define holiness simply by your lifestyle choices.

So, again, what is holiness? When it comes to actually defining what it means, we often struggle. I know I struggle with it. However, in the context of this study, I found something about holiness that is simple—yet amazingly profound. Are you ready for it?

Holiness means being separated unto God. While the term "holiness" carries a strong connotation of moral purity, the most basic meaning of the word is to be "set apart" or "dedicated" to God. In other words, holiness means "to belong to God."

There is a difference between just believing in God and actually belonging to God. I have heard it said that there are three distinctive characteristics of a man or woman whom God calls holy. A holy person is one who believes in God, one who belongs to God, and one who behaves like God. Many people believe in God—at least with their mouths. However, even the demons believe (and tremble). We must go beyond belief. We must realize that we are no longer our own property. We are bought with a price and belong to God. Therefore, we must glorify God and behave like God in our bodies. 1 Corinthians 6:19–20 explains:

> *What? know ye not that your body is the temple of the Holy Ghost which is in you, which ye*

have of God, and ye are not your own? For ye
are bought with a price: therefore glorify God in
your body, and in your spirit, which are God's.

Holiness defines our *relationship* with Him, not just our actions or lifestyle. Referring again to 1 Peter 1:16, we find Peter quoting Leviticus 11:44 when he says:

Because it is written, Be ye holy; for I am holy.

Therefore, we are sanctified (set apart, holy) because of our relationship with God. He is our God and we are His people. Before we are called to do good works, we are called to be holy because that is the definition of our relationship with Him. However, when we try to define holiness by using the Law (Old Testament) without understanding it in the light of our relationship with Jesus (New Testament), we reduce the meaning of holiness to mere morality. That is not enough. Unfortunately, morality can, and does, change with the times and with the culture.

We need something that does not change. When we are born again, we are united with Christ. He *never* changes. As I mentioned previously, it does not mean that we simply believe in Him. Our faith is not only a system of beliefs but it is also a personal, one-on-one relationship with the Creator of the universe. Paul told the Church at Ephesus in Ephesians 2:6:

And hath raised us up together, and made us sit
together in heavenly places in Christ Jesus.

In Christ, we are set apart for His use. His holiness has now become our holiness. We are holy because we are His. Holiness is relationship-based and any definitions of holiness that follow that fact must be grounded upon this very truth. Anything less becomes an ineffective religious exercise based upon works. It might look good on the outside, but it does absolutely nothing on the inside. The Pharisees had this problem. Jesus pointed it out in Matthew 23:27:

> *Woe unto you, scribes and Pharisees, hypocrites! for ye are like unto whited sepulchers, which indeed appear beautiful outward, but are within full of dead men's bones, and of all uncleanness.*

No amount of change to the outside will affect the inside. Yet, Jesus, on the inside, will change the outside. Elisha, obviously, demonstrated this type of change and it was noticeable. This great woman could tell there was something different about him. As he passed by, she recognized the characteristics of a holy man. What exactly were those characteristics? Scripture does not tell us. However, I believe it had to be his behavior. His words, of course, had to be important. But, I believe his life backed up what he said. Think about what people say about us. Can they perceive that we are holy by our actions? Or, are our words simply an empty profession?

When she recognized there was something different about Elisha, the woman said something to her husband. I am sure other people heard about him as well. The thing is that we are all, at some point, the subject of someone's conversation. I know I have been. But, what do they say about us? I know I have, at times, brought shame and reproach to Christ because of my conduct. People love to talk about things like that. Tongues wag when there is some juicy gossip. In reality, tongues wag all the time anyway. I see (and hear) it all the time. 1 Peter 3:16 says:

Having a good conscience; that whereas they speak evil of you, as of evildoers, they may be ashamed that falsely accuse your good conversation in Christ.

We need to live a life that causes those who talk badly about us to be ashamed because what they say about us does not match the example of our lives. We do not always need to be quick with an answer to defend our honor. Let our lives and character do that. Eventually, people will see and will either talk about that or at least stop with the negative talk. Unfortunately, when they stop talking about you, they will move on to someone else. That is just human nature.

But, if more Christians would really live holy lives (and not holier-than-thou lives) in business, school, church, and home, revival would literally break out across the United States and around the world. I really believe that. The biggest ministry is not in the pulpit. It is in the home. Sermons are important. We need the foolishness of preaching! But, living a holy life means more than just preaching a sermon. It means living it each moment of every day. That is what we need. We simply need to live the Christian life.

If we are faithful in serving the Lord and living a holy life, we will see fruits for our labors. Elisha did. He was invited to stay in this home and He was used to bring blessings into this household. We, too, can be a blessing in the lives of others. We do not need to be concerned about the results—that is God's job—but we do need to be faithful. We will reap, if we do not faint.

If we are faithful in our believing, our belonging, and our behaving, our lives will be fruitful to the glory of God. If this occurs, it is only because we are holy—set apart, dedicated to God—and only because of what He is doing in us.

Therefore, holiness is a vital part of the Elisha factor. Because of its importance, holiness is something we should desire. We need to seek it. We need to live it. Holiness defines our relationship with God.

I know I need it. The same is true for you.

Factors to Consider:

1. How do you define holiness?

2. How can we make sure we are living a life of holiness, and not a life of legalism? Is there a difference? If so, what is the difference?

3. Sometimes it is hard to live a life of holiness around family. If asked, what would your family say about you and your Christian faith?

4. Have you seen results from living a life of holiness? If so, what have you seen? If not, what do you trust God to see someday?

5. Even if you are not called to be a formal preacher, how can your life "preach" to others?

Factor Six:
Thoroughly Furnished

2 KINGS 4:8–10

And it fell on a day, that Elisha passed to Shunem, where was a great woman; and she constrained him to eat bread. And so it was, that as oft as he passed by, he turned in thither to eat bread. And she said unto her husband, Behold now, I perceive that this is an holy man of God, which passeth by us continually. Let us make a little chamber, I pray thee, on the wall; and let us set for him there a bed, and a table, and a stool, and a candlestick: and it shall be, when he cometh to us, that he shall turn in thither.

—2 Kings 4:8–10

We learned in the last chapter that the "great woman" of Shunem noticed that Elisha was not just a man of God, but that he was a *holy* man of God. Holiness is essential in the Christian life. It is not optional. God is holy, and, we are commanded to be holy, too.

Because she recognized the importance of Elisha's ministry, she and her husband provided a place for him to stay while he was in the area. They made a room and provided all the furnishings he would need. Scripture tells us they provided a bed, a table, a stool, and a candlestick. They provided the things that were essential for the prophet's comfort as he traveled through the area.

The physical furnishings of this room typify how we should be furnished spiritually. Paul tells Timothy in 2 Timothy 3:17 that we need to be well-furnished, successful laborers for Christ:

> *That the man of God may be perfect, thoroughly furnished unto all good works.*

Hillside Bethel Tabernacle Church, my home church in Decatur, Illinois, has a small house on the campus that is called the "Prophet's Quarters." Early in my life, I actually lived in this very small house for about one year or so. Others have also lived in that house. It served as a "starter home" for many young families for several years. However, in recent years, the house has become the "Prophet's Quarters." Instead of paying for hotels when ministering guests come to town, they can stay in the house. It is fully furnished, including a bedroom, a kitchen with a table and chairs, furniture to sit on, and plenty of lights. Sometimes we have traveling evangelists stay there when they are ministering in the area, even though they may not be at Hillside during that particular visit. We do this to be a blessing to traveling evangelists, pastors, and prophets. It is a comfortable little house.

Why is it important to be fully furnished? Without the necessities, the home will not be as useful. If it is not useful, the prophet will not be as effective in ministry because they will have to expend energy and time meeting their physical needs. The same is true in the spiritual sense. We need to be fully furnished to be effective in our ministry. Over the years, I have learned that the pieces of furniture listed can serve as a powerful object lesson for us.

By providing a bed, the first of the furnishings listed, the woman and her husband made a way for the prophet to rest. This bed came at no cost to Elisha and he could stay there every time he passed through. Have you ever stayed in a hotel? It can be nice, but it can also be expensive. Someone has to pay for the room. In this case, the generosity of the woman and her husband allowed Elisha to find rest at no cost to himself.

For us, we find our spiritual rest in Christ. He paid the price and He is our Sabbath (rest). Jesus taught the principle that the Sabbath rest was instituted to relieve man of his labors, just as He came to relieve us of our attempting to achieve salvation by our works.

Hebrews 4 is the definitive passage regarding Jesus as our Sabbath rest. Without Him, we cannot have true rest or true peace. Isaiah 57:20 says:

> *But the wicked are like the troubled sea, when it*
> *cannot rest, whose waters cast up mire and dirt.*

Second, consider the table that was provided in the room. The table symbolizes a place where people come together to eat and fellowship. Christians are great at this! Elisha needed nourishment and fellowship during his travels just as we need nourishment and fellowship on our spiritual journey. One way the Church celebrates this fellowship with Jesus is through the ordinance of Communion. Jesus desires true communion with us, not just a religious exercise but an intimate relationship.

I remember the story in the Gospels where Jesus communed with His disciples at the Last Supper. The Bible tells us that Jesus desired to spend this time with them before He died. He desires to spend time with us, too. He doesn't just want our service. He wants us to know Him. He is knocking at the door. Will we let Him in so he can come in and fellowship with us?

> *Behold, I stand at the door, and knock: if any man*
> *hear my voice, and open the door, I will come in*
> *to him, and will sup with him, and he with me.*
> —Rev. 3:20

Third, there is a stool. We can use the stool as a symbol of instruction. We cannot be everything God wants us to be if we do not spend time at His feet and receive His instruction. Remember the story of Mary and Martha? Mary would sit at Jesus's feet and receive His word. Martha was busy working. Both are important. However, we cannot neglect the time at Jesus's feet, especially when we use the excuse that we are working for Him. Do we really know what it is to sit at His feet and to learn of Him?

> *But one thing is needful: and Mary hath chosen that good part, which shall not be taken away from her.*
>
> —Luke 10:42

Finally, the fourth essential furnishing is a candlestick. This is the symbol of our testimony. We are, because of Jesus, the light of the world. The Lord wants to shine through us. We should not cover the light nor should we extinguish the flame. Our duty is to let Jesus shine through us in our actions and in our words, and the light shows what is happening on the inside. In the Prophet's Quarters at Hillside, there is a candle in the window. The candle serves as a warning light. If the temperature gets too low in the house, the light comes on. This alerts us to what is happening on the inside. Our light serves the same purpose. It shows what has happened to us. We are changed on the inside and the light illuminates the darkness. When we surrender to Him, He makes us as lights shining in dark places in order to glory Him. Matthew 5:16 tells us:

> *Let your light so shine before men, that they may see your good works, and glorify your Father which is in heaven.*

So, these four essentials for a well-furnished life have everything to do with our personal relationship with the Lord. Our rest is found in Christ. Communion and fellowship is enjoyed with Christ. Instruction is received from Christ. And, our testimony, our light, shines for Christ.

Are you thoroughly furnished?

Factors to Consider:

1. All of the 10 Commandments are upheld in the New Testament, including the Sabbath Day. However, it is not about a particular day, but about Jesus. How is Jesus now our Sabbath (rest)?

2. Communion is an ordinance of the Church. It symbolizes our intimacy with Jesus. What are some ways your personal life shows your intimate, fellowship with Jesus?

3. How do you learn about Jesus? How is church attendance helpful in learning more about Him? How is your attendance? Should you attend more? Why or why not?

4. We are the light of the world. How is your life an example of light in the darkness? Give some practical examples.

5. Elisha needed the help of others in order to be thoroughly furnished. How can others help you in your walk with the Lord?

Factor Seven:
Reviving the Next Generation

2 KINGS 4:18-37

In the last chapter, we learned that the Shunammite woman and her husband provided a thoroughly furnished room for Elisha. Because Elisha needed a place to stay while ministering in the area, this woman and her husband stepped up and provided a blessing to Elisha. As we will see in this chapter, this blessing is returned to the family. No doubt, this is just one blessing (granted, a major one) they received from being around Elisha.

As I contemplated further about "Thoroughly Furnished," I thought how sometimes I feel "Thoroughly Finished" instead. Why is that? I continued to look at the words, the story we had studied, and how I could apply it to my own life. Then I noticed the difference between the words "finished" and "furnished." A couple of letters make the difference. What are those letters? They are "i" and "ur." In other words, I ("i") am the difference and you are ("ur") the difference. Just like Elisha needed the family in order to be fully furnished, we need each other in order to be fully furnished. We are members of the same Body. Therefore, we need each other. If it is just about me ("i"), then I am finished. When I recognize you are ("ur") needed, I can become furnished.

In this story, we see the importance of the next generation. In order to keep moving forward, in order to live the double-portion life, we must be concerned about those who are coming behind us. We must prepare them for their place in the ministry—today. Jesus was concerned about the children. He called the children to come to Him (sometimes to the dismay of His disciples). We must do the same as Jesus. Notice the phrase in 2 Kings 4:26 where Elisha asks, ". . . is it well with the child?" We must look at the world and the Church today and ask, "Is it well with the children?" If not, we need to take the appropriate steps to revive this generation.

> *Run now, I pray thee, to meet her, and say unto her, Is it well with thee? Is it well with thy husband? Is it well with the child? And she answered, It is well.*
>
> —2 Kings 4:26

By asking the question (and not just rhetorically), we can measure the condition of our children. In the case of the Shunammite's son, he was not well at all. He had died. I am not sure why she said, "It is well." We are clearly told in verses 20 and 32 that the child had died.

Gehazi, Elisha's servant, spoke as though maybe the boy was sleeping. In reality, though, he was dead.

What about our children? I am not talking about the physical well-being of our children now. Remember, Old Testament stories, while real, provide spiritual examples for us today. Think about what happens in our Sunday Schools, our Children's Church, our Youth Groups, and our summer Youth Camps. What is the spiritual status of our children? Are they alive? Are they sick? Are they dead? Again, we are talking about spiritual things.

Quite naturally, the boy's mom was concerned. Her concern moved her to action. Any parent would try to move heaven and earth to physically save their children. Do we have the same passion about spiritual matters? If so, why are our youth groups not much more than a party, a concert, or a mere get together? Do we have real concern for the salvation and spiritual conditions of the young people in our care? We say we do, but the proof is in the action. The Shunammite woman took action. Are we really taking action?

The Shunammite woman hurried to find Elisha. Gehazi, Elisha's servant, tried to keep her away, but Elisha told him to leave her alone. Elisha, the holy man of God, did not know why she had come. He could tell something was wrong, but he didn't know what. This tells us that God does not always reveal everything to us. Some things we have to learn in the natural order of things. We cannot be so "super spiritual" that we forget that we live in a natural world. Elisha learned there was a problem and he immediately sent Gehazi ahead to lay his staff on the face of the child.

Gehazi arrived and, as instructed, he placed Elisha's staff on the face of the boy. And then...nothing happened. Huh? Why not? What is the lesson here? Well, it seems to me that Gehazi had some problems. We will learn a lot more about him in other chapters. For now, I see a lack of preparation. He went to work without seeking God. He did not pray. He was not prepared. Therefore, nothing happened. Preparation precedes blessings. It is a Biblical principle. We must pray, fast, and even travail sometimes in order to see the blessings of God. It seems as though Gehazi had no prayer, no preparation, no persistence, and no faith. It is no wonder he had no results.

How many youth leaders, Sunday School teachers, or Children's Church directors just wing it? I have heard the following excuses:

"There isn't enough time to prepare."

"I am busy."

"I work a full-time job."

"I am a volunteer; I am not paid to do this."

"This is not my priority. I have a family."

"I have other responsibilities."

These excuses may even have some truth or reasonableness to them. If we are not careful, though, our service can become a formality. We sometimes want the position, but we do not want the responsibility. We have a form of godliness, but we deny the power.

This is going to be a strong statement, but it is said in love. If you are not willing to prepare, then step aside. Let someone who has a passion for children step in. There is no disgrace in acknowledging a position is not for you. The disgrace is in going through the motions, seeing no results, and thereby doing our children a great disservice. Do not let your service be just a formal matter. Thankfully, Elisha arrived on the scene. He showed up, assessed the situation, and took charge. And, he began with prayer. Before he could minister life to this young boy, he had to be in touch with God himself. Are we praying regularly and diligently for our children? If not, we should not be surprised when we do not see results. I cannot emphasize enough the importance of prayer before we engage in ministry to others. Whether it is with children, adults, saved, lost, or whatever or whomever the audience, always prepare for ministry with prayer.

Next, Elisha had personal contact with the boy. To be sure, it is an odd scene to imagine and some may be crass in their description of what happens. Some may even be grossed out by it. But, again, remember we need to apply spiritual principles to what we are learning. What does Elisha do? 2 Kings 4:34 says that he "lay upon the child, and put his mouth upon his mouth, and his eyes upon his eyes, and his hands upon his hands."

If we are going to effectively minister to the next generation, we must be:

1. **Mouth to mouth.** This means we must be able to speak their language. In order to revive the next generation, we must be able to communicate with them.
2. **Eye to eye.** This means we must see things from their perspective. It is easy to impute our perspective upon others. In order to be effective, we must see where they are coming from.

3. **Hand to hand.** This means we must be involved in things that interest them. What are their hands doing? Where are their feet going? Can we identify with their world and engage them right where they are?

Of course, all these things must line up with the Word of God, but we cannot let generational differences come between us. That means we, as adults, must be willing to put aside our preferences (think of music, think of activities, think of dress, etc.) and be willing to establish real contact with those we are seeking to impact for the Lord. I have learned the best way to influence someone is to first allow myself to be influenced by them in some way.

Elisha displayed preparation and contact, but he also displayed an intense desire with effort. He demonstrated patience and perseverance. This miracle did not happen all at once. Elisha had to hang in there. He had to keep his faith in God, and he had to keep pressing. Maybe we sometimes fail because we get impatient. We give up when we should be pressing in. We stop believing when we need to keep trusting God for the victory. Aren't our children worth it?

Elisha thought so. He hung in there. The child began to warm up. He sneezed seven times and then he opened his eyes. He revived.

Our children are dying (or may already be dead) spiritually. Do not give up and certainly do not just go through the motions like Gehazi. Preparation precedes blessing. Ministry is work. Yes, it is hard work.

Do not take it lightly. The next generation is counting on us.

Factors to Consider:

1. Is it well with the children of your family and/or Church? Explain your response.

2. How have you (or leaders of your Church) prepared to minister to the children?

3. When was the last time you prayed, earnestly prayed, for the children of your family and/or Church?

4. Are you willing to identify with the next generation, even if it does not line up with your preferences? Explain your response.

5. Have you, or someone you know, just gone through the motions of service? How can we correct this disservice to our children?

Factor Eight:
Having Abundance

2 KINGS 4:38–44

One of the greatest promises of the Christian life is that God will supply all of our needs. Some have perverted this promise by trying to make God like some magic genie that appears to grant our wishes. I remember a genie that would appear in a popular children's cartoon.

[Genie appears in a puff of smoke]—"What do you need?"

However, God is not obligated to give us our wishes and our desires. He is not our magic genie. He does promise, though, that He will give us what we need. When our desires line up with His, our desires are also granted. The key is aligning with God.

I remember a story about Abraham Lincoln when somebody was inquiring whether God was on the side of the Union. President Lincoln's response was that we should not expect God to be on our side but rather that we should be on His! How true!

When we are on His side, He will supply all our needs according to his riches in glory by Christ Jesus (Phil. 4:19). Maybe we do not get our wants, but He will give us what we need. In this chapter, we see provision and abundance supplied to the School of the Prophets that was located in Gilgal.

We are told that there were about 100 students in this school, who are described as "the sons of the prophets." There was a famine in the land and these students were in danger of starving. As we expect, a wonderful thing happened. A man arrived on the scene with a gift for Elisha. However, Elisha instructed that it be given to the students. When he did, they were all miraculously fed. There was even some left over!

Does this sound familiar? It should. Jesus performed a couple of miracles just like it. Remember the story of the "Feeding of the 5,000?" It can be found in Matthew 14:13–21. Likewise, the "Feeding of the 4,000" can be found in Matthew 15:32–39.

Therefore, we see both Old and New Testament examples of the promise that God provides for the needs of His people. How does He do this? Let's use the story found in 2 Kings to provide us with some factors we can use.

First of all, God gives provision according to His word. In other words, when God says something, you can count on it. The power is not in the promise. The power is in the One keeping the promise. We can count on God to keep His Word. In 2 Kings 4:43–44 we see "thus saith the LORD" and "according to the word of the LORD."

And his servitor said, What, should I set this before an hundred men? He said again, Give the people that they may eat: for thus saith the LORD, They shall eat, and shall leave thereof. So he set it before them, and they did eat, and left thereof, according to the word of the LORD.

I have heard the phrase "thus saith the Lord" misused many times. In an effort to give a little extra weight to a prophetic word, I have heard people add these words to the end of the proclamation. Now, I am *not* treating prophecy with contempt and I am *not* saying that prophecy does not occur. It does. I have been witness to it. But these phrases are not "magic" words to give the message a godly "seal of approval." If God says it, it will happen whether we add the tag line or not.

Not one of God's promises has ever failed. Not one. That is because God does not fail. He always keeps His word. He *must* keep His word. It is a part of who He is. The psalmist says in Psalm 138:2:

I will worship toward thy holy temple, and praise thy name for thy lovingkindness and for thy truth: for thou hast magnified thy word above all thy name.

Therefore, when God says He always provides for His children, we can be assured that it is true. It may not be the way we want or expect. Nevertheless, it is still true.

Second, God provides in response to our prayers. Even though God says He will provide, we still need to pray. Why? Is there power in prayer? Well, not exactly. Now, stay with me here. I am not saying that prayer is not important. We must pray. However, the power is not in the prayer. Otherwise we could pray to anyone or anything. There is power in the One to whom we pray. When we pray, we are demonstrating our dependence upon Him. Prayer does not make God more willing to answer because He already wants to answer. Prayer just provides the conduit through which He *can* answer. The provisions of God come via answered prayer—either our own prayer or the prayer of someone else.

Third, God provides at the appropriate time. I know, this can sometimes be extremely frustrating. I want the answers when I want them. God, however, does not necessarily work on the same time schedule that I do. While this sometimes frustrates me, He knows what I need and He knows when I need it. He will provide it at the appropriate time—not a second sooner or later.

And, God provides in a meaningful way. God provides exactly what we need. If we need food, He will not necessarily give us money to buy food. He may make another way to receive it. Be open to alternative answers to prayer. God can do amazing things! No matter what, though, you can trust Him. What are your needs—your real needs? Ask Him for help. Then, watch Him provide!

Fourth, God provides from unexpected sources. Do not be surprised if your answer comes from a source you never expected. In the story, we know nothing about this man from Baalshalisha (2 Kings 4:42). Who was he? Where did he come from? Why didn't God use a familiar character? Why a complete stranger? Who knows? Just know that God provides. Elijah was fed by ravens. Elijah was also sustained by a widow. These were unique sources for sure! God has resources far beyond our wildest imaginations and those sources never dry up. He never has to figure out a way to supply our need.

Fifth, God uses people. Not only does God provide from unexpected sources, often times those sources are people. Think about that. Do you realize that YOU can be the source that God uses to help someone? We pray for blessings. We pray for miracles. But, we also can be the blessing. We can be the miracle. Allow God to use you.

Last, God provides abundantly. God is not the God of just enough. There was plenty of food left over. It was a miracle! Someone provided the source, but God multiplied it. What God gives you is more than enough. Again, I am not talking about hyper-faith and that we will have all that we want and then some. However, I do believe that the blessings of God are more than we need, particularly when we realize that we have Him (and He has us). What more do we need?

Oh, I want to point out one more thing. Elisha was not selfish. The gift was brought for Elisha. He could have kept it for himself. But, he didn't. He shared it with the students. When we are given blessings from God, we need to share it with others. Do not hoard it. Share it. The more we give, the more he gives. The more He gives, the more He would have us give. That's just who He is. So, that's what we need to be—givers!

The psalmist said, "The Lord *is* my shepherd; I shall not want" (Ps. 23:1). How true. We can live our life—abundantly.

> *The thief cometh not, but for to steal, and to kill, and to destroy: I am come that they might have life, and that they might have it more abundantly.*
> —John 10:10

Factors to Consider:

1. Why is it important to align with God's desires instead of expecting Him to align with yours?

2. Has God ever answered a prayer of yours differently than you desired? How did you react?

3. If God knows what we need before we even ask, why do we still need to pray?

4. Has God ever used an unexpected person or resource to answer a need in your life? If so, explain what happened. If not, do you now think maybe God did but you just missed realizing it?

5. God is a giver, so we should also be a giver. How are you a giver to others? Do you need to give more? Explain.

Factor Nine:
Dealing with Sin

2 KINGS 5:1–27

I think the story of the cleansing of Naaman is perhaps one of the most popular stories connected with the ministry of Elisha. I remember this story from my childhood and have heard it told many times. I even heard a sermon called, "Seven Ducks in a Muddy River." See what the preacher did there? Well played, sir. Well played!

This story is popular because within the narrative we find an allegory of the condition of man. More specifically, we find the condition of each one of us individually. I am not speaking about an infectious, gross, *physical* condition. Rather, I am speaking about an infectious, gross, *spiritual* condition—**sin**.

Throughout Scripture, we find many illustrations of sin. Of them all, the condition of leprosy stands out the most to me. It stands out to me because I have psoriasis, an incurable skin disease. Some scholars have believed that leprosy, as described in the Bible, may have been psoriasis.

Some believe psoriasis to have been included among the skin conditions called "tzaraat" in the Hebrew Bible, a condition imposed as a punishment for slander. The patient was deemed "impure" during their afflicted phase and was ultimately treated by the kohen, a member of the priestly class. However, it is more likely that this arose from the use of the same Greek term for both leprosy and psoriasis. The Greeks used the term "lepra" for scaly skin conditions. However, they used the term "psora" to describe itchy skin conditions. Leprosy is distinguished by the regular, circular form of patches, while psoriasis is always irregular.

Whether psoriasis is the same as leprosy in Bible is unclear. Although, I do believe that what we commonly think of leprosy today (Hansen's Disease) is not necessarily the same as leprosy mentioned in the Bible. Whatever the actual disease, it was (and is) a grievous malady. It is not something anyone wants to have. The stigma attached to it is alienating, depressing, and quite loathsome. Naaman had it, and he needed to get rid of it.

Sin is the same way. We all have it. It is alienating (from others and from God), depressing, and quite loathsome. Like Naaman, we need to get rid of it. While it seems there is no cure, there is One (and only One) that can be found. As it was for Naaman, so it is for us. The Bible tells us in 2 Kings 5:1:

> *Now Naaman, captain of the host of the king*
> *of Syria, was a great man with his master, and*

honourable, because by him the Lord had given
deliverance unto Syria: he was also a mighty
man in valour, but he was a leper.

I find this description of Naaman interesting. He was a great man. He achieved many great things, things of great importance. I am sure he was courageous, popular, and dependable. He had a lot going for him. But…

There is always a "but" in the story, isn't there? As good as Naaman was, he was a leper. Beneath his beautiful garments, his medals, and his successes, there was the loathsome disease of leprosy. We are all like that. We may have success in this world. We may be looked at with admiration and awe. Even so, beneath it all is tragedy and sorrow. I am sure that Naaman tried to hide it. I have tried to hide my psoriasis. It embarrasses me. It makes me feel unworthy and less of a person, which is a terrible side effect. The emotional turmoil that comes with psoriasis can be worse than the disease itself. Sin is the same way. We try to hide it from others. But, it is still there. God sees the heart. 1 Samuel 16:7 says:

But the Lord said unto Samuel, Look not on
his countenance, or on the height of his stature;
because I have refused him: for the Lord seeth
not as man seeth; for man looketh on the outward
appearance, but the Lord looketh on the heart.

This is the condition of us all. I know, we are generally decent, kind, and moral people. Right? Well, we at least try to be that way. As hard as we try, though, we still have sinful hearts. We, without the Lord, are spiritually diseased. We can try to cover it up and pretend that it is not there. But it is.

> *For all have sinned, and come short of the glory of God.*
>
> —Rom. 3:23

Thankfully, Naaman had a maid in his house (kidnapped from Israel, by the way) who told him there was an answer to his leprosy. I think sermons could be preached about this maid. Think about how you would feel about someone who captured you and made you work as a servant. I would probably laugh at his calamity and say that he deserved it. But, she had compassion on him. We need to be like this maid—willing to testify to the healing power of God to our enemies! I am speaking of the spiritual healing we need, not just our physical bodies. We need to share the answer to the sin problem, even to those against us.

Because of this maid, Naaman went to Israel to find the cure he desperately needed. The king of Syria arranged this trip for him because Naaman listened to the advice of the maid. Well, that is not entirely correct. You see, Naaman made some mistakes. He did not listen completely. He thought he could buy his healing. He took with him a great deal of money. But, all the money in the world could not cure him. Money cannot cure us of sin, either. We may think we can earn or buy our salvation. However, God is not impressed. Salvation is a gift. There is nothing we can do to purchase it. We can do nothing at all.

The other mistake Naaman made was that he went to the wrong place. He went to the king when he should have gone to the prophet. How many people today are knocking on the wrong door trying to find salvation? We try false religions, good works, or spiritualism. But, there is only ONE way. Jesus is the way. Going through another will not work. It just won't.

The final mistake Naaman made was that he wanted to be healed in his own way. He became mad when he learned of God's method of cleansing. Elisha's instruction was to dip seven times in the Jordan River. What? Naaman was looking for something big and demonstrative. He was looking for fanfare. He did not even get to speak to Elisha directly. How rude! He was a big deal, so he was looking for a big deal.

We do the same thing. We go to church looking for the clouds to part, the sun to shine through stained glass windows, and the sound of an angelic choir to fill our ears. We despise the day of small things. We get mad if the pastor fails to shake our hand. We want big and we want awesome. We want recognition and when we do we can easily miss out because we can miss God. We often worship the fanfare (our worship) more than we worship God.

Once again, Naaman had some servants who could speak the truth to him. If Elisha had told him to do some great thing, he would have done it. So, why not do this small thing? What did he have to lose? Naaman decided to go and dip seven times in the Jordan, just as he was instructed. Seven is the number of completion and he was not healed until he dipped the seventh time.

The Jordan River has great symbolism, too. We often equate crossing Jordan to dying and going to heaven. However, the correct interpretation is thinking of the crossing of the Jordan as symbolic of entering into the Christian life—the Promised Land. We cross the Jordan as we are cleansed by the Blood of Jesus. As the old hymn says, "O, precious is the flow, that makes me white as snow."[1]

To receive his healing, Naaman had to humble himself. He had to be obedient. Then, and only then, was there a cure. The same is true for us. If we want to get rid of the sin in our lives, we must humble ourselves. We must be obedient to Christ.

Unfortunately, the story does not end here. Gehazi, Elisha's servant, was up to no good. Gehazi followed after Naaman and deceived him into giving Gehazi some of the gifts that he had brought. Gehazi returned and Elisha confronted him, but he lied to Elisha. Elisha was not fooled and immediately called him on it. There is something about the phrase that Elisha uttered in 2 Kings 5:26 that gets to me every time:

> ...Went not mine heart with thee, when the man turned again from his chariot to meet thee?

We can be sure our sins will be found out. I have been caught. How about you? I wonder what Gehazi was thinking. Remember the incident with the raising of the young boy? When the woman arrived, Elisha did not

---

1 Robert Lowry, "Nothing but the Blood," 1876.

know why she had come. Perhaps Gehazi thought there was no way Elisha would know about this. But, he does. Oops. He is caught in his sin.

We started this story with leprosy, which means we started this story with sin. There was a great healing that took place. A wonderful miracle occurred. However, we end the story back in the same place we began. And, so it is with life. We see victory after victory. But, the battle is not over. Sin has a death grip on people, even people in the church. Our battle is not with people, but with sin.

Sin brings consequences. Gehazi and his children were stricken with leprosy. Instead of being washed white as snow, he left a leper as white as snow. Wow, what irony. It is not a funny irony. It is sad. Unfortunately, this story is too familiar as it happens every day.

When we inherit the double portion, we still have to deal with sin. There is a cure. But, it must be done the right way—Yahweh—not my way.

Factors to Consider:

1. What is sin?

2. Explain how every person is guilty of sin, no matter how "good" or "great" we are.

3. Do you ever find yourself looking for a "big deal" or expect special treatment/recognition? How can God use the "small things" to minister to you?

4. Why is obedience important when we are dealing with sin?

5. If Jesus died once and for all, why do we still have to deal with sin today?

Factor Ten:
Flying Off the Handle

2 KINGS 6:1–7

The story of the recovery of the lost axe head is found in 2 Kings 6:1–7. I have often heard this story and, while interesting, was never really able to draw a spiritual parallel. Oh, I know about the importance of taking care of borrowed items. My dad always taught me to return something as good as it was (or better) than when I first borrowed it. The same thing applied to using a vehicle or room. Clean it up. I was to make sure it was like I found it. If possible, I was to make it better than when I found it. This is all very good advice and has a lot of practical application.

However, as I read this story again, I was searching for something deeper. Yes, these practical lessons still apply and still should be heeded. But, is there something more here? I think there is.

As I previously stated, I believe that Old Testament stories are for our example. They are for our example in the natural. They are for our example in the spiritual. What spiritual lesson can we find here? Here is the text as found in 2 Kings 6:1–7:

> And the sons of the prophets said unto Elisha, Behold now, the place where we dwell with thee is too strait for us. Let us go, we pray thee, unto Jordan, and take thence every man a beam, and let us make us a place there, where we may dwell. And he answered, Go ye. And one said, Be content, I pray thee, and go with thy servants. And he answered, I will go. So he went with them. And when they came to Jordan, they cut down wood. But as one was felling a beam, the axe head fell into the water: and he cried, and said, Alas, master! for it was borrowed. And the man of God said, Where fell it? And he shewed him the place. And he cut down a stick, and cast it in thither; and the iron did swim. Therefore said he, Take it up to thee. And he put out his hand, and took it.

This is interesting. It is certainly not every day that we hear about a piece of iron floating like that. Even the unsinkable Titanic, which was made of iron, sank. As the crew discussed their fate and whether the ship would sink, it was stated, "She's made of iron, sir! I assure you she can . . . and she will."[2] So, hearing that an axe head, made of iron, could swim is quite miraculous!

------

2. *Titanic*, directed by James Cameron (1997; CA: Paramount Pictures), DVD.

In this story, I see an analogy of the Christian life. Elisha represents Jesus, and the sons of the prophets represent Christians. The axe head represents power. More accurately, it represents the enabling of the Holy Spirit to work in our lives. It is not our power. It is God's.

This, to me, is a message about those of us who have known the power of God in our Christian service, but have now become ineffective. Somehow, we have lost our head and have flown off the handle. We have a form of godliness, but in the middle of our service we have somehow lost the power. Thankfully, this story also gives us the example of restoration!

The sons of the prophets wanted to be around Elisha. They desired to dwell with him and they wanted a relationship with him. It reminds me of the relationship between Elijah and Elisha. This, too, is essential in our service to Christ. Fellowship and communion with Him is vital. He must be a part of what we are doing. Otherwise, everything we do is in vain. These men also showed that they had a burden about the need for service. They had to do something. They had to work and they were anxious to get busy.

Elisha saw this and he commissioned them to do the work. He said, "Go ye." Do you see any similarity to something else in Scripture? Didn't Jesus commission the disciples in Matthew 28:19? He said, "Go ye," too. However, it was not enough for them to go alone. The sons of the prophets needed Elisha to go with them. Jesus also promised that He would be with us—always! We need His abiding presence in our Great Commission!

Go ye therefore, and teach all nations, baptizing them in the name of the Father, and of the Son, and of the Holy Ghost: Teaching them to observe all things whatsoever I have commanded you: and, lo, I am with you always, even unto the end of the world. Amen.

—Matt. 28:19–20

And so they went. Everyone worked. They were energetic. They had the right tools. They work together, with Elisha, on the task at hand. Everything was going great. Until...

It happened. Something broke down. It never fails, does it? One worker was working and lost his axe head in the process. Without it, his effort was useless. He had to stop working. Without the right tools, he would be ineffective and, perhaps, even dangerous. I do not think this worker was evil, nor do I think he meant to lose the axe head. Yet, it happened anyway.

Have you ever lost your head and flown off the handle while working? It can happen if we are not careful. Just like losing an axe head, it can be a gradual process and not just an instantaneous event. What do I mean? Well, axe heads do not generally just fly off. They often work themselves off with each swing until the final swing sends it flying.

I have worked with an axe several times. I remember needing to stop periodically to make sure the head was not working its way off. I had to pound it back on and then continue working. Or, sometimes I needed to stop and rest a little bit to make sure my swings remained accurate. An inaccurate swing could result in the handle breaking and the axe head could go flying. That can be extremely dangerous for anyone around.

However it happened, the worker lost his power. Unfortunately, the axe wasn't his. It was borrowed. Our tools, our talents, and our abilities are not ours, either. We are stewards. They belong to God (see the Parable of the Talents in Matthew 25:14–30). He immediately noticed the loss and he was distressed about the loss.

Too many times, some people act oblivious when this happens. They keep on working. Not only are they ineffective, they can also be dangerous. They can look pretty foolish, too. Have you ever lost your axe head? You used to know God's power resting upon you. Could it be gone because you did not do the correct things to maintain it? Maybe it is lost. Maybe the blade is dull. If you keep on working, you will be ineffective. It is okay to stop, realizing there is an opportunity to be restored and reinstated. It is possible to be reequipped for service.

First, as I already stated, we need to stop when we lose the axe head. Continuing on without the power of God is dangerous and foolish. Then, we must make a full confession to Jesus. The worker immediately stopped and cried out to Elisha. If we fail, must make a full confession of our failure to the Lord. He is faithful and just to forgive!

Believe it or not, this is not the first example of an axe head flying off the handle in Scripture. Deuteronomy 19:5–6 gives us this example:

> *As when a man goeth into the wood with his neighbor to hew wood, and his hand fetcheth a*

stroke with the axe to cut down the tree, and the head slippeth from the helve, and lighteth upon his neighbor, that he die; he shall flee unto one of those cities, and live: Lest the avenger of the blood pursue the slayer, while his heart is hot, and overtake him, because the way is long, and slay him; whereas he was not worthy of death, inasmuch as he hated him not in time past.

In these verses we see that God made provisions for "cities of refuge." These cities would provide safety for those who were innocent of premeditated misdeeds. In other words, this was an accident. However, it was not uncommon for the family members of a slain person to exact revenge on the person who killed him, even if it was an accident. Therefore, God provides some relief from this primitive system of justice.

It is not difficult to see some definite spiritual parallels to Christ in these cities of refuge. The person who caused the death had to get to the city of refuge. He had no time to lose. Once there, he had to declare his cause to the elders. In other words, he had to confess what happened and own up to his mistake. And, it had to be real repentance. Otherwise, the elders would turn him over to the "avenger of blood."

That is what happens in this story, too. The worker had to tell Elisha what happened and had to show him where it took place. We must be completely honest with the Lord and show him where we lost our effectiveness and our experience of His power in our life. He knows. But, we need to know, too, and, we need to be open about it. 100% transparency. Have you failed the Lord? Have you lost your head and flown off the handle? If so, where did it fall? Find the place. Tell the Lord. You will never recover your axe head until you tell Him where (and how) you lost it.

Then, the miraculous happened. Elisha used a stick (a piece of wood) to recover the axe head. This is important because the way back to God is through the cross. It is the only way. But, the story does not end there. The man had to put out his hand and recover the axe head as it swam to the surface. Likewise, we must reach out in faith and accept what God is recovering in our own lives.

Everyone falls and everyone fails at some point. Sometimes the failure is caused by sin and other times the failure is caused by an honest mistake. This is not the whole issue or problem. The issue is whether we immediately stop what we are doing and run to our own City of Refuge—His name is Jesus. This story gives us a picture of this type of restoration. Thank God for His restorative power in our lives. The definition of success is simply standing up one more time than you fall down.

> *For a just man falleth seven times, and riseth up*
> *again: but the wicked shall fall into mischief.*
> —Prov. 24:16

Factors to Consider:

1. Name some examples in your life of how you are obeying the Great Commission.

2. How should fully understanding that Jesus is always with us impact our daily activities?

3. What talents/abilities do you have that are "on loan" from God? Are you using them?

4. When we lose our effectiveness, why is it important to stop for a season?

5. Where in your life have you ever lost your effectiveness? What did you do about it? Are there any areas of your life today that are ineffective? What do you plan to do about it?

Factor Eleven:
Looking Beyond What You Can See

2 KINGS 6:8–23

When my daughter was small, we watched many Disney movies over and over again. Among her favorite movies was *The Lion King*. I used to be able to quote this movie nearly line by line.

As with many popular movies, there were sequels, which are almost always not as good as the original. However, *The Lion King 1 1/2* did provide a very interesting line. While looking for the perfect place to live, Timon was told to "look beyond what you can see." Timon took this literally and thought the perfect place to live was just beyond Pride Rock. He went there and life did seem perfect, for a while. Later, he came across Simba and found that his life has a deeper meaning. Then his eyes were opened and he understood his purpose.

In this story, we see a similar situation. Elisha's servant must look beyond what he can see. The enemies of Israel also have a problem with eyesight. It can happen in our faith walk, too:

> *For we walk by faith, not by sight.*
> —2 Cor. 5:7

Israel was experiencing hostilities with the king of Aram (Syria). Invading parties would make border raids against the Jews. Later, an organized Syrian army invades. But, for now, plundering parties tormented Israel. Elisha, however, would somehow spoil these raids. Each time they planned to invade, God would give a revelation to Elisha. Elisha would inform the king of Israel and they would take precautions against these invasions. This frustrated the Syrians and the king thought they had a traitor among his troops. However, he quickly learned that Israel had a prophet who knew the king's plans, even while he spoke of them in secret.

In order to be successful, the king of Syria decided he had to murder Elisha. Why he thought he could pull this off when he wasn't successful with his previous schemes is baffling. The decisions we make while influenced by sin are not always logical. Nevertheless, he sent an entire army to surround Elisha at Dothan and he surely intended to kill him.

In 2 Kings 6:15, our story gets interesting. Elisha's attendant went out oblivious to what was going on. He didn't immediately know about the enemy (although he quickly discovered it). Likewise, he didn't know about

God's provision. This day was one like any other. It was business as usual and he was taking care of his daily assignments. This servant had no mind or concern for the battle around him. This meant he was completely unprepared for what he faced. Sound familiar? How often do we get caught off guard by the enemy—our spiritual enemy?

Too often we do not take our spiritual warfare seriously. We go out unprepared. Yes, we have daily tasks to complete, but we must always be prepared spiritually. If not, our reaction will be much like Elisha's servant. We cry, "What do I do? What do I do?" Fortunately, the servant sought the counsel of the prophet. He went to the man of God. Today, we often seek other sources for answers. Generally, we keep seeking until we find the answer we want to hear. It's crazy. But, I sometimes do it, too. Or, we post it on Facebook and hope that we will somehow get the answer we need. How quickly we listen to the advice and voices of the world rather than meditate on the Word!

In a striking contrast, Elisha was prepared. This was no surprise to him. He was focused on God's surrounding armies who were far greater in strength and numbers. Therefore, Elisha was calm, relaxed, and confident in the Lord his God. Because he was prepared, he was able to help deal with his servant's fear. He did this in three ways: (a) he showed personal concern through a word of encouragement, "Do not fear," (b) he gave biblical instruction on why he should not fear, "for those who are with us are more than those who are with them," and (c) he prayed for his servant and asked the Lord to "open his eyes that he may see."

This is a powerful example for us today. We can minister to the fears of people just like this. However, we must be prepared. When we are prepared, we can show personal concern, give biblical instruction, and go to the Lord in prayer. Our tendency, however, is sometimes to neglect one or more of these three steps. Either we are impersonal and cold in our teaching and in our relationships, or we may be very friendly but fail to communicate God's truth. Sometimes we trust in our own abilities and skill and we fail to pray. Leaving out any of these steps can be dangerous and not helpful.

The response of the servant shows us how fear can paralyze us. The problem was not that the servant saw too much. The problem was that he saw too little. He only had eyes to see the problem or danger. Now, seeing the problem and danger is not wrong. In fact, I believe it is necessary. Some Christians walk around and act like they do not see problems or danger. They say, "If I confess it then it becomes real." Hello! It IS real. It IS there. Recognizing a problem is not the problem. Not seeing God as the answer is the problem!

Have you ever seen a child close their eyes and act like you cannot see them because they cannot see you? We laugh at the silliness of this game but we do the same thing. It is all right to say we are sick if we are indeed sick. We just recognize that we have a God bigger than our sickness. It is no wonder the world makes fun of Christians. We walk around oblivious to real life happening around us. We think if we "see" it then it will have some sort of power over us. But, if we do not see it, everything will be fine. Wake up! Grow up! See the problem. But, make sure you also see the solution. Look beyond what you can see. Stand still and see the salvation of the Lord! We need the eyes of faith to see and believe God for the fact of the dangers Satan and his hosts may bring against our lives. We need eyes of faith to believe God for the fact of His divine presence, His sovereign plan, and His provision.

Open the eyes of my heart, Lord! I want to see YOU!

Elisha could see and he was delivered. In a twist, the eyes of his servant were opened and the eyes of his enemies were blinded. Elisha prayed and asked the Lord to strike his opponents with blindness so they might not see (or perhaps recognize) the prophet. This prayer was answered and Elisha led them into the city of Samaria and into the hands of the king of Israel!

He brought them there to show them the power, wisdom, and mercy of the God of Israel. He could have caused their destruction, but he did not. By his acts of mercy and abundant provision he sought to convince, convict, and maybe even shame them. But, he did not kill them.

The direct effect of this was to bring about an end of the raiding bands. The king of Syria would later lay siege to Samaria with an army. So, the king wasn't stopped. However, it appears this act of mercy did have some effect on the people who participated in the raids. They stopped.

Satan will never stop attacking. Nevertheless, the way we treat and interact with people can make a difference. The spiritual battle will rage on, but we can still directly impact people. Our battle is not with them.

When Paul wrote to the Church of Ephesus in Ephesians 6:12, he said:

> *For we wrestle not against flesh and blood, but against principalities, against powers, against the rules of the darkness of this world, against spiritual wickedness in high places.*

Therefore, we need to show mercy to people. Understanding we are involved in spiritual warfare is an important factor. In order to do that, we must look beyond what we can see.

It is okay to see the problem. Just make sure you see the God that is for you, too.

Factors to Consider:

1. Describe a time when you have been so busy with "religious duties" that you missed seeing the "spiritual battle" that was about to take place. What was the result?

2. How can we always be spiritually prepared? Is it really possible?

3. Elisha encouraged his servant. Why is encouragement an important factor? What else did Elisha do for his servant?

4. Does recognizing a problem demonstrate a lack of faith? Does verbalizing a problem make a problem so? Why or why not?

5. Why is it important to recognize that our true enemy is NOT other people? How can the way we treat those who are against us impact their relationship with us in the future?

Factor Twelve:
Finding Blessing in Trouble

2 KINGS 6:24–8:29

The final episodes in the life of Elisha begin in 2 Kings 6. For most of Elisha's ministry, peaceful conditions existed. Raiding bands had tormented Israel. However, Elisha's wise decision (as seen in the last chapter) put an end to that. Nevertheless, a full-out siege eventually took place and Samaria was hit hard.

As we know, God promised Israel that he would bless her for obedience to His covenant. He also promised a curse if they disobeyed. This message was reinforced by both the ministries of Elijah and Elisha. During Elisha's ministry, there was a temporary lull in the external attacks upon Israel. Perhaps God was attempting to show His grace and mercy. However, as per usual, there was no evidence of repentance by Israel or her kings. God, in keeping with His Word, withdrew His protective hand and Israel faced a full-scale invasion.

This invasion must have lasted a while. The Bible records that a famine, perhaps due in part to the invasion, meant that little meat was available. A donkey's head was able to be sold for about two pounds of silver! Even though it was considered unclean, the people resorted to eating donkey meat and even the least edible part of the donkey became very costly. It gets worse. While walking along the wall, the king comes across a case of cannibalism. Even this atrocity did not bring the king to repentance. Instead, he blamed Elisha and swore to see him put to death. 2 Kings 6:31 says:

> *Then he said, God do so and more also to me, if the head of Elisha the son of Shaphat shall stand on him this day.*

In his anger, the king dispatched a messenger to kill Elisha. Not long afterward, the king realized he had made a mistake, and he ran after the messenger to stop him. However, Elisha, by divine insight, already knew about the king's plans and he had men bar the door until the king (Jehoram) could stop the execution. Elisha must have known that the king changed his mind because they held the door until the king arrived.

When the messenger arrived, he admitted the current troubles represented the judgment of God. Instead of trusting in the Lord for deliverance, it seems the king was ready to throw in the towel. He must have felt that things were so helpless that there was no other solution than to surrender to the Syrians.

Have you ever felt that way? When we come to our senses and realize the trouble we have brought on ourselves, sometimes the feeling is so overwhelming we want to give up. We want to throw in the towel. While recognizing our sin, we continue to sin by failing to trust God for deliverance. Yet, God is a God of grace and mercy. Even when we fail, even when we sin, He is there to help. We just have to rely upon Him. We have to see that, even in the middle of trouble, an opportunity for God to intervene exists.

God can still bring deliverance. In fact, Elisha told the king that it would come the very next day. Perhaps the king believed it because the Bible does not record that he said anything in reply. He must have called off the order to kill Elisha. But, the king's officer scoffed at this prophesy. He was skeptical of the whole thing. Elisha confirmed the truth of the prophecy but also added to it. Elisha said that the officer would see it with his own eyes, but he would not get the opportunity to partake of the deliverance. This serves as a warning to us all. When we fail to believe the promises of God—when we fail to see the opportunities in trouble—we fail to experience the blessings of God.

We also see the opportunities of blessing and restoration to the Shunammite woman. 2 Kings 8:1–6 gives us this story. While the royal officer scoffed at the promise of God, this godly woman believed the prophetic word given to her. She acted on her faith and she obeyed by leaving the country and escaping the famine. When she returned, she found others living on her land. She appealed to the king and, after hearing of her story (as told to the king by Gehazi), the king restored to her all that was hers. Even in the middle of trouble, she found God's blessings.

That's the way life is. Even though we may seem unsuccessful, our prayers unanswered, our work unrewarded, we are never unloved. God does care and He is involved in every aspect of our lives. We may not be able to avoid the trouble, but we can still find blessings in the middle of it. It may not be now. It may not be in the way we expect. But, if we endure and hold to the promises, I believe we will see the reward.

In a stark contrast, we see one other person who tried to find blessing in trouble. The problem is that this person's motive was very self-serving. 2 Kings 8:7–15 tells us about Hazael and his treason. The king of Syria (the enemy of Israel) had fallen ill. Remember, this is the king who tried to capture and kill Elisha. However, in his time of need, he sent word to Elisha (along with a gift) and inquired about his possible recovery. Even our enemies, though they may not repent, will respect our honor and integrity as we minister the Word of God.

While the king, Ben-Hadad, wanted Elisha to restore him to health, Elisha's involvement is related to the Lord's instruction to Elisha to anoint Hazael to be king over Syria instead. Hazael was waiting for Ben-Hadad to die so he could assume power. When he arrived, Elisha told Hazael that the king would recover from his sickness. However, he also told him that the king would die. That seemed like a riddle and double-talking but, once again, Elisha knew exactly what was going on. He knew Hazael's character. He knew that he was waiting in the wings for the king to die.

Elisha stared steadily into the eyes of Hazael until Hazael was ashamed. But, Elisha's gaze soon turned to weeping. He wept because he knew that Hazael would inflict great hardship on Israel. Despite Hazael's protest to the contrary, this indeed became the case.

When Hazael returned to the palace, he gave the good news. The king would recover. However, Hazael smothered the king and assumed the throne. This evil person found an opportunity in trouble, too. But, he used it for his own gain, for his own power, and for his own ego.

There are opportunities all around us, even in times of trouble. The question is this: Are we seeking God's blessings or are we seeking to take advantage of others? The character of our heart will reveal our motives. Our words may say one thing, but our actions will show what is really going on in our heart. God wants to bless us. We just have to believe His promise and trust His Word. We must act in faith, believing God will see us through the trouble. Taking matters into our own hands will cause destruction, hardship, and even death.

Are you like the king of Israel, the king of Syria, or the Shunammite woman? Each had opportunities in trouble. Only one was able to fully realize God's blessings.

Factors to Consider

1. How do times of trouble fit in with God's promises? What can be the determining factor between blessings and curses?

2. Name a time you wanted to "throw in the towel" because of trouble. What did you actually do? Did you quit? Why or why not?

3. Name a time God provided deliverance when it did not seem possible. How did you respond?

4. The Bible says, "Despise not prophesyings" (1 Thess. 5:20). Have you ever been skeptical of prophecy? What is the difference between despising prophecy and testing whether the prophecy is true?

5. Have you ever taken matters into your own hands in an effort to make something happen? If so, what was the result? Would it have been better to wait on the Lord? Why or why not? Is there ever a time to take matters into your own hands?

Factor Thirteen:
Leaving a Legacy of Life

2 KINGS 13:14–21

The final days of Elisha are recorded in 2 Kings 13:14–21. All the way up to the end (and even after his death), God used Elisha to demonstrate His power. There are many things we did not cover in this book. I encourage you to read about these miracles, too. I believe the reason for all of these events was to get Israel's attention. God was calling her to repentance and to faith. Elisha was the messenger of God. And the miracles authenticated the message of God.

While we sometimes focus on the miracles in the Bible, we really need to focus on the message. Unfortunately, we often look for the experience or the miraculous. All the while, we should look for the message. Since miracles do not happen everywhere we look (that is why they are called miracles), we need to pay attention when they do occur.

I believe God uses the supernatural manifestation of His Spirit to draw attention to the message that we need to hear. If we focus on the miracle, we are easily discouraged when it fades away. If we focus on the message (and heed the message), we will not be discouraged because God's Word does not pass away. The generation of wickedness and adultery follows the signs. In contrast, God's people have signs *follow them.*

> *A wicked and adulterous generation seeketh after a sign; and there shall no sign be given unto it, but the sign of the prophet Jonas. And he left them, and departed.*
> —Matt. 16:4

> *And these signs shall follow them that believe; In my name shall they cast out devils; they shall speak with new tongues; They shall take up serpents; and if they drink any deadly thing, it shall not hurt them; they shall lay hands on the sick, and they shall recover.*
> —Mark 16:17–18

Are you a part of the wicked and adulterous generation or a part of the chosen generation with the double portion? Signs authenticate the message for the New Testament believer. They did for Elisha, too. This is his final story. . .

Elisha fell ill. It was a terminal illness and he was going to die. Elisha had performed many miracles in the past. He even raised the dead. Given everything we have seen, healing his own sickness should have been an easy miracle. Yet, this illness is not a problem. Dying is okay because it was time to die. Ecclesiastes 3:1–2 says:

> *To every thing there is a season, and a time to every purpose under the heaven: A time to be born, and a time to die; a time to plant, and a time to pluck up that which is planted.*

As we have studied, Elisha influenced many people, including kings. His influence went as far as Israel's enemy. Now that is real influence! As word got out about Elisha's illness, the king of Israel (King Jehoash) paid Elisha a visit. I think the king realized he was about to lose a great asset, and the king realized Elisha's superior position by calling him "my father" in true humility.

The king had served Yahweh, but not completely. This was a problem with most of the kings of Israel. Yet, I believe he recognized the Lord was the real defense and power of Israel. He recognized that Elisha was His prophet. Therefore, he knew things were about to change and it would affect his power and influence dramatically.

Elisha had been a tower of strength to the nation. The king would miss him and the king would mourn him. However, I believe he was so dominated by his power and authority that he refused to let the message truly change him.

This happens today, too. How many presidents had great respect for the late Rev. Billy Graham? Most, if not all, in recent history. Now, how many presidents have been changed by the message Billy Graham preached? If their actions are any indication, very few.

Why are presidents and politicians unchanged by the message of the Gospel? Because we, the people, are unchanged by the Gospel. Our government is from the people, by the people, for the people. Our leaders are a reflection of us. In other words, we have reaped what we have sown. We have ignored the message. We get what we deserve.

King Jehoash was no different. He ignored the message. Even so, Elisha instructed the king to pick up his bow and shoot toward Aram. Elisha explained this act meant that Jehoash would win a total victory. He then instructed the king to strike the ground with arrows. This showed that the divine promise that was just stated was to be augmented by the king's personal participation. And so, the king obeyed, but he only did it three times. Instead of using the five or six arrows that were available, he limited his participation to three.

Elisha became angry with the king. Had the king used all his arrows, he would have completely vanquished his enemy. Now he would only gain three victories. Isn't that like us? When called to participate in the divine, we often only do it halfway. We do not go all out and we do not give it our all. We expect God (or someone else) to do the work. It is no wonder we do not experience more victories in our own lives when we do things halfway.

Therefore, the king had to live with the consequences of not fully understanding the message. With this pronouncement, Elisha's earthly ministry was complete. He soon passed away.

In total, it appears that Elisha's ministry spanned something around 56 years. He was laid to rest wrapped in linen clothes. In all likelihood, he was probably buried in a cave or a tomb hewn out of a rock. He was mourned but life went on. A while later, some men were burying a friend nearby and they were surprised by a group of raiders. Perhaps in fear of their own lives, they quickly opened up Elisha's tomb and tossed in the body. As soon as the corpse touched Elisha's bones, it immediately came back to life!

Even in Elisha's death, we see the miracle of resurrection. We see the legacy of life and we see, in Elisha, a glimpse of the ministry of Christ. What we do for the Lord will last, even after we are dead and gone. Our actions today can bring life to our friends, families, and maybe even strangers long after we are gone. But, we have to live with eternity in mind. We have to leave a legacy of life. That is what Elisha did.

Consider the miracles we have studied. Remember, miracles must validate the message. What is the message in the miracles from the life of Elisha? The Gospel is the death, burial, resurrection, and soon return of Jesus. Now, go back and look at some of the miracles we have studied: (1) the raising of the Shunammite's son, (2) the healing of Naaman, (3) the miraculous multiplication of the food, (4) the recovered axe head, and on and on it goes all the way up to our final story in this chapter. The emphasis on the Resurrection and the hope found in Jesus is the message in the miracles! Every event prior to Calvary points forward to the Cross. Every event after Calvary points back to the Cross.

For I determined not to know any thing among you, save Jesus Christ, and him crucified.

—1 Cor. 2:2

Today, do we need miracles in order to believe the message? Not really. Remember the story of the rich man and Lazarus in Luke 16:19–31? The rich man wanted a miracle by having someone return from the grave to warn his family. Abraham answered, "If they hear not Moses and the prophets, neither will they be persuaded, though one rose from the dead" (Luke 16:31).

Miracles will not convince. Only the heart's willingness to listen and believe the message will suffice. We are not changed by miracles. We are changed by the message. That is the only thing that will truly persuade us. We need God's message of love and grace that is manifested in the work of Christ and revealed by the Holy Spirit in our lives.

If we want to leave a legacy of life, we need to live the message of the Gospel.

That is the Elisha factor, and that is living the double-portion life.

Factors to Consider

1. Even people of faith fall ill and will ultimately die. Does this represent a "lack of faith" on the part of the believer? Why or why not?

2. Take a moment to examine your life so far. Are there examples of you doing things halfway for the Lord? What are they and what are you willing to do about it?

3. How have we "reaped what we have sown" regarding our national leaders?

4. What are things that you can do to leave a legacy of life to those who are coming up behind you? Think of your children, your grandchildren, and the children in your church.

5. Only the message of the Gospel will change us, and not miracles. What is the Gospel message? Summarize it in your own words that you can share with someone today.

NOTES:

NOTES:

NOTES:

CPSIA information can be obtained
at www.ICGtesting.com
Printed in the USA
FFHW011131311018
49182402-53378FF